THE RIGHT

RISK

AND

CRISIS MANAGEMENT PLAN

THE RIGHT RISK

AND

CRISIS MANAGEMENT PLAN

By

Saad E. Abbas

P ISBN: 978-1-7392159-6-5
E ISBN: 978-1-7392159-7-2
Year: 2022

Published by
Gulf Book Service Ltd
20-22 Wenlock Road, London
NI 7GU
UK
Email: info@gulfbooks.co.uk

Designed by: New Tech FZE

Consultant, Trainer, Mentor and Author

Saad E. Abbas

MBA, RACMC, CLC, CCMC, CIC, FGLC, SGC, ECMC, CCEPRM, AFIIBI, RMIFIC, DEIB (Finance), ICDL, MAD, QMS-LA, MBAD, DQA-TL, SKEA-TL, ADAGEP-TL, IAA-A, DHDA (Assessor Trainer), BIT & BLSI (ASHI), BLST & ALST (AHA), NAEMSE, MFAI & Ml (PADI), IT (ISEA), HSAI (HSA)

Degrees and Certifications:

- MBA (Financial Wealth Management) University of Hull UK.
- Risk and Crisis Management Consultant (RACMC)
- Certified Life Coach (CLC)
- Certified Career Management Coach (CCMC)
- Certified Innovation Consultant (CIC)
- Future Government Leader Consultant (FGLC)
- Smart Government Consultant (SGC)
- Event and Conference Management Consultant (ECMC)
- Certified Consultant in Electronic PR & Media (CCEPRM)
- Associate Fellow Institute of Islamic Banking & Insurance (AFIIBI)
- Risk Management Islamic Financial Institutions Consultant (RMIFC)
- Dubai Quality Award (DQA), Sheikh Khalifa Excellence Award (SKEA), Abu Dhabi Award for Excellence in Government Performance (ADAEGPTL) Team leader.

Work Experience:

- 20 Years Experience in Banks (National Bank of Dubai – ABN AMRO Bank – Barclays Bank – Emirates Bank International)
- 20 Years Experience as a Government Consultant, Trainer, Coach and Mentor

Training Programs Conducted:

1. Mastering Risk and Crisis Management
2. Mastering The Perfect Interview
3. Mastering Customer Service
4. Mastering Virtual Meeting Etiquette
5. Mastering Change Management
6. Mastering Feasibility Study
7. Mastering Conflict Management
8. Mastering Innovation Management
9. Mastering Business Plan Writing
10. Mastering Leadership

Author:

1. How to Get the Right Job in 2007
2. The Right Resume and Curriculum Vitae
3. The Right Interview
4. The Right Virtual Meeting Etiquette
5. The Right Risk and Crisis Management Plan

CONTENTS

1

The Difference Between Risk and Crisis Management?

The main important thing to remember about the difference between Risk and Crisis Management is:

- Risk management is mainly concerned with identifying, assessing and justifying any activity or event that could cause harm to a business before the problem could occur.

- Crisis management is mainly concerned with responding to, managing and recovering from an unforeseen event that could cause immense problems for the business or even cause the business to fail after the problem has occurred.

<table>
<tr><td>Risk Management

Before the Problem
has occurred</td><td>Crisis Management

After the Problem
has occurred</td></tr>
</table>

What Do You Do Before the Creation of the Plan?

The most important thing to start with is assessing what risks can affect your organization. There are 2 types of risks.

1. Internal Risks: are basically problems that could occur within the organization like departmental risks. Each department within an organization could face problems. It is your job as a Risk and Crisis Management expert to list these problems, and find suitable solutions to these problems before they turn into a crisis.

   Examples of internal risks: Computer system crash, loss of data due to negligence or old computer systems servers, key staff members exiting the organization, decreased performance levels, being understaffed, lack of communication, poor teamwork, budget problems, failing to meet Deadlines and many others.

2. **External Risks:** are basically risks that come from outside the organization and these risks are very dangerous, if no plan has been put into place the business could fail.

   Examples of external risks: Computer virus, Ransomware, Natural disasters (Earthquakes, Floods, Tsunami's, Tornadoes, Hurricanes, Wildfires, Drought and others), changes in government legislation, economic risk, competitive risks, interest rate hike risk, new technology risk and many others.

First: List all the Internal Risks

Create a list of all the internal risks that the organization could face. Make the list department-wise. List each department and what could go wrong within that department. This list could be long that is ok as each department has its onset of potential problems that it could face.

Second: List all the External Risks

Create a new list with all the external problems that the organization could face. Remember departmental risks are small and easy to solve but external risks are big and have a problem by being expansive to create risk management plans. As each external risk has its own set of problems.

As a risk and crisis management expert it is your job to identify the risks and find suitable and cost-effective plans to solve the risks before they can turn into a Crisis. Or have a plan in place even if the disaster occurs the effects of that disaster will be very minimal.

NOTE: The true importance of risk and crisis management is to be ready for whatever problems that could occur in the future with a tried and tested plan.

What to Do Before Creating the Plan

Before creating the Risk and Crisis Management Plan there are a few steps that must be followed.

1. **What is the overall risk appetite of the organization?**
    Many large organizations create a risk appetite report or statement. This document helps to guide organizational risk management activities. A risk appetite statement includes a focus on the ability level of the organization to withstand risk and the measures in place that have been planned to withstand any major risk.

-   **Acceptable Risk Boundaries and Actions:** Risk boundaries are what the organization is willing to do within acceptable risk boundaries, that are connected to the level of cost and staff needed to handle the risk.

-   **Risk Exposure:** Based on a researched set of actions and risk outcomes, risk exposure to any possible risk issues or difficulty can increase, decrease or stay the same, the level of risk exposure influences the risk appetite of an organization in relation to the approach taken by the organization and the overall direction in terms of the budget to solve the risk issues. Is the amount and number of staff budgeted for this problem enough to solve the problem or not? If **NO**, then the risk appetite is low if **YES** then the risk appetite is high.

- **Analysis of Long-term Objectives:** An organization should create a long-term risk appetite list of what issues have the low risk appetite and what issues have a high-risk appetite and accordingly plan for each issue that is in line with the strategic goals and objectives of the organization.

2. **How to write a risk appetite statement:**

The risk appetite statement should be created considering all concerns of all stakeholders that address all the implications and current organizational plans and strategies. This also means that the need for constant review of these strategies, plans and practices should be a part of the risk management plan.

It is very important to be able to consider the organizational culture and the overall emphasis regarding risk tolerance and risk appetite.

It is important to be able to define all acceptable levels of uncertainty or volatility in risk situation that is apart of the risk appetite statement.

The reconciliation of the risk appetite and risk tolerance with the risk exposure based on current plans and financial budgets.

It is very important to safeguard the plans put in place in the risk appetite statement that is applicable to the organization's needs. It is important to state where, how and when any plan will be applied.

3. **Examples of risk appetite in practice:**

- An organization is not willing to accept any risks that could result in loss of revenue or a drop-in sale. Such as a high percentage of defective products. Bad product reviews from customers, increase in customer complaints.

- Some organizations are very comfortable in putting customer and staff data on the cloud. But are less willing to put the organization's financial data on the same cloud. The question is if the organization is happy with the security a cloud provider is providing for customer data. Why are they not happy to use the same security for financial data? Isn't customer personal information important to the organization?

- The risk appetite of any organization should be fixated on the level of risk that the organization is willing to take in accordance with its goals and objectives, at the same time keeping economic, political cultural and environmental factors in mind.

4. **Does the organization have systems to react to changes in the level of risk that may affect the organization?**
   Types of changes that could affect the organization. Like new competitors in the market, new laws that could affect business, new taxes that were not accounted for and newer models of products with better specifications, that make your products obsolete.

   It is important to have a system in place that recognizes any changes, that were not accounted for, that could affect the organization in a negative way. Creating such a system is very important for any organization it could also have a cost involved. A better way of doing this is Risk Prediction.

What is Risk Prediction?

Risk prediction is very important to be able to predict a potential problem before it ever becomes a problem and solve it, this is being proactive. Example: traffic. If the data I have shows me that every morning between 6:30 am and 7:30 am I have an increase in traffic on a particular road. What should I do to solve this problem and what are the costs involved?

Some organizations purchase insurance, against any unforeseen risks, this protects them from any risks that were not planned or budgeted for. When purchasing insurance, it is very important to go over what is covered and what is not covered in the insurance policy. Sometimes organizations fail to check the policy and what they thought they had insured against turns out that the policy does not cover. So be very careful when purchasing insurance for your business. Small businesses need insurance because any unforeseen risk could actually close the company.

The Speed of Response in a Crisis Situation

In any crisis situation, the speed of response is the most important. It all depends on how fast you as an organization can recover from the crisis. The slower you respond to the crisis the higher the financial loss is. If you look at companies who responded slowly and companies who responded quickly how did it affect the bottom line?

EXAMPLE NO. 1:

Merck drug manufacturer needed 2 years and 11 months to review the effects of its Drug Vioxx in 2004, this delay caused a huge drop in the share price of Merck of –46%.

EXAMPLE NO. 2:

On the afternoon of 2 deaths Johnson and Johnson halted all product marketing, they sent 450,000 messages to hospitals and clinics to stop subscribing to the Drug Tylenol, they setup a hotline for anyone who needed more information. This cost the company US$ 100 million. This was one of the greatest recalls of a drug in history all the drugs were removed from the shelves within hours. The government officials said that this was excessive and that 2 deaths did not determine that the drug was dangerous. Johnson & Johnson issued warnings to its customers not to take the painkiller Tylenol in 1982. The share price of Johnson & Johnson dropped only 9.5%.

Despite evidence that the poison was introduced via store shelves, Johnson & Johnson did not try to evade blame. The company became a pioneer in developing tamper-proof packaging and eventually moved away from capsules to a more tamper-resistant caplet. In less than a year, Tylenol regained its market share and sales leadership, it continues to rank highly for consumer trust.

EXAMPLE NO. 3:

In August 2005, Hurricane Katrina hit the U.S.A. Gulf of Mexico Coast and flooded the city of New Orleans, causing more than $100 billion in property damage and killing more than 1,800 people. Even though the hurricane began as a natural disaster, the scale of the catastrophe was man-made. An analysis of the response, including a report by Congress, focused on weak aspects of crisis management and highlighted the following important lessons:

- Preparation is Key to any Crisis response
- Training the Crisis Management Team is very important
- Clear communication between all crisis management team members is very important.
- To act quickly but not rashly—all actions have to be pre-planned according to the scenario. As every crisis has more than one scenario so must the crisis management plan have more than one response scenario.

EXAMPLE NO. 4:

In March 2018, a British firm called Cambridge Analytica bought data from about 87 million users and their friends without their consent from Facebook. The company used the data to build voter profiles that Cambridge sold to election campaigns, including Donald Trump's presidential campaign.

This sparked a scandal over user privacy at Facebook, the biggest of many. CEO Mark Zuckerberg was called to testify before Congress. The company faced investigations by regulators in the United States and Britain, as well as lawsuits from several jurisdictions.

The financial repercussions included the following:

- The U.S. Federal Trade Commission imposed a US$5 billion fine against the company—the largest ever. The FTC said Facebook's behaviour violated a previous consent decree with the agency. The Securities and Exchange Commission fined the company US$100 million and British regulators fined Facebook GBP 500,000.

- Engagement on Facebook dropped by 20 percent in the months after the scandal, a metric that affects the company's ad revenue.

- Facebook users' confidence in the company dropped 66 percent in the weeks after the scandal.

- Growth in Facebook revenue and users dropped in the quarter after the Cambridge Analytica affair. The company's stock valuation lost US $130 billion in two hours after the news, weakening the social network's forecast further.

This is an indication that the faster an organization responds to a crisis the lower the losses and the faster the recovery. It is very important to be fast when responded ng to a crisis situation.

Sources of Information

- https://www.techtarget.com/searchsecurity/definition/What-is-risk-appetite
- https://www.ventivtech.com/blog/how-to-perform-a-simple-business-risk-assessment#:~:text=Business%2Drisk%20assessments%20identify%20potential,pressing%20need%20for%20these%20assessments.
- https://asana.com/resources/crisis-management-plan
- https://www.smartsheet.com/content/crisis-management-examples

The Risk and Crisis Management Plan

The framework analyses of risk and crisis management in three phases:

- Preparedness before a crisis and involves activities aimed at developing capacities that will assist in effective anticipation, response and recovery from a crisis.
- Response to limit damages once the crisis occurs.
- Clear feedback after the crisis through feedback mechanisms that review, analyze and draw lessons from the actions taken to mitigate the damage.

What have we learnt after COVID 19?

COVID-19 Lessons: From Crisis Management to Recovery

- From a pandemic comes an opportunity
- Preparing for the unexpected
- A readiness to make key decisions comes from proper support and training
- The importance of coordinating a single approach
- From crisis management to business continuity

The 10 Risk and Crisis Management Steps to Creating the Perfect Plan

1. The creativity and originality of the idea
2. Explanation of the expected crisis

3. The plan and the objectives
4. Choosing the best response for your organization
5. Choosing the risk and crisis management team.
6. Choosing the best partners to implement the plan
7. Who are the targeted groups and how to segment each group and why
8. What are the communication channels and how to choose the best channels for your plan.
9. What are the key resources to implement the plan.
10. The timeline for creating the plan.

1. The Creativity and Originality of the Idea

How innovative is the idea—it should be different from any similar ideas—how original is the idea—finally who is the originator of the idea.

How innovative is the idea?
It is very important that the idea be innovative. The more innovative the idea the more chances are that the idea will be implemented. Yes, some people will say keep your ideas simple; but let me ask you this how many simple ideas get implemented?

The idea should be different from any similar ideas.
You may find similar ideas in your organization. But ask yourself this how similar the suggested idea is to my idea. Are there any differences.

Who is the originator of the idea?
If you find an idea that is like your idea simply state this. An idea by (Person's Name) was suggested previously and gives a brief explanation of that person's idea.

It is important to be sure that the idea hasn't been applied previously, or has it?
Before you recommend a risk management plan be very sure that such a plan has not been implemented within the organization or suggested previously by one of your colleagues or a colleague who has left the organization.

If you start working on a plan and the plan had been suggested previously and had been rejected, then you have wasted all your time over nothing. Plus, your colleagues will tend to distrust you that you have stolen someone else's idea and claimed that it was your idea.

It is important to know that there are any similar ideas to your idea, if you find any similarities:

- **What are the similarities?**

  As stated previously you must state the similarities between your idea and the idea that was presented previously and was rejected. This will show the listeners that you have thoroughly done your research and you understand the situation. This will also show everyone that you are an honest person and that you do not steal people's ideas and claim they are your ideas. **Remember honesty is always the best policy.**

- **What are the differences?**

  The second step you must now state the differences what makes your idea greater than the previous idea. This is where you must sell your idea to the listeners. You must state each and every difference with conviction and that these differences make your idea better than the previous idea or ideas and implementing your plan will be beneficial to the organization as a whole.

  Remember that the most important difference in your idea is your greatest selling point so you must maximize the selling aspect of that main deference and convincing people that your idea is the best possible action to be taken is very important for the organization and for you as you will be the project manager.

- **What is the Idea?**
  - Is the idea for your division or for another division in your organization?
  - Is the idea for your organization or for another organization?
  - Is the idea for a private business or for a government organization?
  - Is the idea for an international organization—possibly the United Nationals is it a humanitarian Idea?

Remember all these questions are legitimate questions and you must think about each and every question before you start working on the idea. Presenting your idea to the wrong.

2. Explanation of the Expected Crisis

- **Detailed explanation of the Expected Crisis.**
  It is very important to give an explanation of the expected crisis. What are the expected dangers and ramifications of the crisis and what could be the possible causes of the expected crisis.

- **The steps that will lead to the crisis.**
  What are indicator steps that must take place before the crisis becomes a crisis situation. These indicator steps are very important as it helps the organization take quick actions before the crisis turns into a catastrophe. So list all these indicator steps and be very clear when explaining each indicator.

- **The current organizational strategy if any?**
  What is the current crisis management strategy the organization has? Like 90% of most organizations are, no such strategy exists. It is funny how top management view risk and crisis management. They think it is a waste of money and time. But when a crisis happens, like COVID 19 these same top management who were opposed to spending money on Risk and Crisis management plans did not know what to do and most lost their jobs. Not only did many organizations closedown but many people lost their jobs as well. Sometimes spending a small amount of money can save an organization millions, or even save the organization from bankruptcy.

  The larger organizations have the ability to withstand some crisis situations, but the problem is with the small companies that can't afford to spend money on a risk and crisis management plan. They are the ones who are most susceptible to crisis situations, and we witnessed this first had when many small companies closed down during the pandemic lockdown.

- **The plan to manage the crisis is it in line with the organizational strategy?**
  Every large organization has a strategy that it follows, some employees may disagree with the strategy but that is what the top management has agreed to. But that is not our concern. Our concern is my risk and crisis management idea is in line with the organizational strategic plan or not.

  If my plan is in line with the organizational strategy, then I do not have a problem. When presenting the plan, I should state the organizational strategy and how my plan is in line with that strategy. This will help in convincing the listeners that the plan presented is the right plan for the organization.

- **The crisis management plan if not in line with the organizational strategy what is the justification that this plan is better?**
  The problem is when the plan is not in line with the organizational strategy. How do you convince your listeners, that your plan is the best plan for the organization and that it should be implemented even though it is not in line with the mission and the vision of the organization.

  The question is how to convince your listeners that your plan should be implemented?

  - Give people a reason to listen to you talk about your plan

  - Show management that you truly care about the organization and the organization's needs.

  - Give your listeners a very good reason to trust you.

  - Present your ideas in terms of pros and cons that will connect with your audience. I mean what are the positive points about your idea and what are the negative points about your idea.

  - Define the action steps that will be taken and clarify the process. Now that you have convinced your listeners that they should implement your plan, you now have to explain the action plan the steps they have to follow to implement the plan. You have active something great you have motivated your listeners to accept change. Now that the difficult part is over you must now show them how they will implement change, you must remove any ambiguity. Everything must be clear.

What happens with many people is they start with a great presentation, but then they fail to follow through they live their listeners with a new clear direction. This is why many great ideas didn't get implemented. If you fail to define the action steps or clarify the steps that should be taken. All your efforts will be wasted.

3. The Plan and The Objectives

What are SMART Goals?

Goals are part of every aspect of business/life and provide a sense of direction, motivation, a clear focus and clarify importance. By setting goals, you are providing yourself with a target to aim for. A SMART goal is used to help guide goal setting. SMART is an acronym that stands for **Specific**,

Measurable, **Achievable**, **Realistic and Timely**. Therefore, a SMART goal incorporates all of these criteria to help focus your efforts and increase the chances of achieving your goal.

- **Specific SMART Goals**

  Goals that are specific have a significantly greater chance of being accomplished. To make a goal specific, the five "W" questions must be considered:

  1. **Who:** Who is involved in this goal?

  2. **What:** What do I want to accomplish?

  3. **Where:** Where is this goal to be achieved?

  4. **When:** When do I want to achieve this goal?

  5. **Why:** Why do I want to achieve this goal?

  For example, a general goal would be "I want to lose weight." A more specific goal would be "I need to exercise 4 times a week for 2 hours per day to get in shape."

- **Measurable SMART Goals**

  A SMART goal must have criteria for measuring progress. If there are no criteria, you will not be able to determine your progress and if you are on track to reach your goal. To make a goal measurable, ask yourself:

  1. How many/or how much?

  2. How do I know if I have reached my goal?

  3. What is my indicator of progress?

For example, building on the specific goal above: I need to exercise 4 times a week for 2 hours per day to get in shape. Every week, I should lose 1 kg of body fat.

- **Achievable SMART Goals**

  A SMART goal must be achievable and attainable. This will help you figure out ways you can realize that goal and work toward it. The achievability of the goal should be stretched to make you feel challenged but defined well enough that you can actually achieve it. Ask yourself:

  1. Do I have the resources and capabilities to achieve the goal? If not, what am I missing?

  2. Have others done it successfully before?

- **Realistic SMART Goals**

  A SMART goal must be realistic in that the goal can be realistically achieved given the available resources and time. A SMART goal is likely realistic if you believe that it can be accomplished. Ask yourself:

  1. Is the goal realistic and within reach?

  2. Is the goal reachable, given the time and resources?

  3. Are you able to commit to achieving the goal?

- **Timely SMART Goals**

  A SMART goal must be time-bound in that it has a start and finish date. If the goal is not time-constrained, there will be no sense of urgency and, therefore, less motivation to achieve the goal. Ask yourself:

  1. Does my goal have a deadline?

  2. By when do you want to achieve your goal?

  For example, building on the goal above: On January 1st, I will join the gym next to my house. I need to exercise 4 times a week for 2 hours per day to get in shape. Every week, I should lose 1 kg of body fat. At the end of March, I should have lost 12 kg of body fat

4. Choosing the Best Response for Your Organization

How do you know that the presented plan is the best plan for your organization?

- **A quick review of all the suggested ideas.**
  It is very important to list all risk and crisis management ideas presented by your colleagues. At the end of the list present your idea. When listing the ideas, it is very important to list the name of the person after each idea, this shows that you are a considerate person who has conducted a very though research and you wishes to give credit to everyone who has taken the time to think of a possible solution to a potential problem that the organization could face in the future.

  This way the listeners will have a complete picture of what the employees think, and this will support your idea. As so many people feel that it is important for the organization to create a risk and crisis management plan for this particular potential problem. Sometimes top management needs a wakeup call. Looking at so many ideas will give Top management a legitimate reason to look into the matter more seriously.

- **A justification why the other plans will not work or are not feasible.**
  Now is the time to give a justification why each of the plans presented by your colleagues has been rejected. It is important to fully explain why you have rejected each and every idea. You can create a matrix to show the ideas and the reason for rejection. That way it will be clear to your listeners, and you can present it in a faster way without wasting your listeners' time.

Risk Ideas Matrix

Type of Risk	Owner Name	Potential Cost	Positive Points	Negative Points
Risk Idea 1	*Name 1*	Amount 1	1. Positive Point 2. Positive Point 3. Positive Point	1. Negative Point 2. Negative Point 3. Negative Point
Risk Idea 2	*Name 2*	Amount 2	1. Positive Point 2. Positive Point 3. Positive Point	1. Negative Point 2. Negative Point 3. Negative Point
Risk Idea 3	*Name 3*	Amount 3	1. Positive Point 2. Positive Point 3. Positive Point	1. Negative Point 2. Negative Point 3. Negative Point
Risk Idea 4	*Name 4*	Amount 4	1. Positive Point 2. Positive Point 3. Positive Point	1. Negative Point 2. Negative Point 3. Negative Point
Risk Idea 5	*Name 5*	Amount 5	1. Positive Point 2. Positive Point 3. Positive Point	1. Negative Point 2. Negative Point 3. Negative Point

- **A justification why your chosen plan will work and is as per the organizational strategy.**
  Now is the time to show that your idea is the best idea. How do you do that? As you have done previously in the risk ideas matrix. Write your idea, your name, the potential cost, the positive points the negative points. Here you must state the durability of your idea. That means that it can withstand the test of time. That means that even after 10 years your idea will still be the best choice. So, it is not just a temporary solution to the expected potential problem but it is the best solution at any given time.

  The initial cost of setting up the risk management plan is more than justified with the expected benefits of managing such a potential plan, that will make the yearly expenses very negligible as the reduction in the risk turning into a potential crisis is minimized. Thus, saving the organization from possible bankruptcy and the employees from becoming unemployed. This is a very powerful selling point of your idea.

5.   Choosing the Risk and Crisis Management Team

Who are the Team Members?

The Risk Manager

The Risk Manager's main job is to provide an overview of the project's risks and opportunities as well as the modification plan for all risks, this facilitates management's decision-making. They are the central figure for the project's risk management activities.

The Risk Manager has only one job and that is managing all the risk projects with the organization. The risk manager has no other duties to perform as this job is very time consuming.

The Risk Owner

The Risk Owner is responsible for a particular risk within a department. Every department will have their own risk owner. They work together with the risk manager as they have the technical information on the risks and opportunities within their department.

The risk owners could be the originators of the risk management plan with their respective departments. They will have the necessary technical information to work on the plan. It is very important for the risk manager to communicate with the risk owner to a regular basis this will help them modify the plan with new information as and when they obtain it.

The Project Manager

The project manager works in collaboration with the risk manager. The main task of the project manager is to manage individual risk management plans, they set expectations and justify the plans made by the risk manager on the process and status for their individual projects.

The project managers must have a global vision of the risks and opportunities of their project. One of their roles is to place themselves on the important risk response strategies proposed by risk owners, their main duty is to keep the response team ready and fully trained for any crisis that may arise in the near or feather.

The Enterprise Risk Management Team

It has been observed that large organizations most likely have an enterprise risk management team who manages risks at an organizational level. Similar to the risk managers, the enterprise risk management team provides an overview of the organization's risks and opportunities their main task is to ensure compliance with the organization's risk management process.

This requires project risks to be flowed up to the portfolio level for the team to effectively manage enterprise risk. The enterprise risk management team is essential for large organizations to maintain a consistent and effective process for managing risk across the entire organization.

6.   The Best Partners to Implement the Plan

Your partners who will help you implement your idea.

- **Who are your partners?**
  Risk management teams need internal and external partners. Internal partners are other departments that could complement with managing the risk. But our main concern is external partners. Who are they? How did we choose them? What due diligence have we conducted? When choosing a partner, it is very imperative to conduct due diligence. A due diligence check involves careful investigation of the economic, legal, fiscal and financial circumstances of a business or an individual. This covers aspects such as sales figures, shareholder structure and possible links with forms of economic crime such as corruption and tax evasion. A check of this sort is necessary as soon as a company initiates **relationships with a business partner** to join together in a Risk management plan.

- **How will they contribute to the implementation of the idea?**
  This is the moment to think about what these new partners can bring to the organization. How will the organization benefit after joining with any of these new partners. Every new partner you join with has a set of new benefits that they offer and sorry to say they also have a set of badged problems they will bring with them. As an organization, it is your job to search out what organizations benefit out ways its badged problems.

  Once you find that ideal partner then by all means go ahead and join with them as the relationship should be a long relationship. When thinking about risk management then any potential partner should be considered as a partner for no less than ten years of partnership. Any partnership that is deemed to be less than 10 years then the argument for partnering with them should be very clear as to why partner with them for less than 10 years.

- **Why did you choose this organization as your partner?**
  Once you have chosen a partner you must explain why this new potential partner has been chosen over all the other potential partners that were in consideration for partnership. The matrix provided below will help explain to your listeners what each potential partner can bring to the table and what the organization actually needs. Sometimes we do not fully understand our exact needs, so we end up partnering with the wrong partner who does not provide exactly what we need. We may

choose a big-name partner for prestige. But does this big-name partner provide the service or product I need?

Sometimes a small name partner is a perfect fit for the organization, but we overlook them as they are a small company, not a prestigious large famous organization. This is the mistake most companies do and end up wasting time, money and energy over a partnership that should have never been made. Look at the matrix below and follow the steps, be very clear that you will choose the right partner according to compatibility not prestige.

Risk Management Potential Partners List

Potential Partners	Potential Value	Cost of Partnership	Positive Points	Negative Points
Name 1	What can they do for us	Amount 1	1. Positive Pont 2. Positive Pont 3. Positive Pont	1. Negative Pont 2. Negative Pont 3. Negative Pont
Name 2	What can they do for us	Amount 2	1. Positive Pont 2. Positive Pont 3. Positive Pont	1. Negative Pont 2. Negative Pont 3. Negative Pont
Name 3	What can they do for us	Amount 3	1. Positive Pont 2. Positive Pont 3. Positive Pont	1. Negative Pont 2. Negative Pont 3. Negative Pont
Name 4	What can they do for us	Amount 4	1. Positive Pont 2. Positive Pont 3. Positive Pont	1. Negative Pont 2. Negative Pont 3. Negative Pont
Name 5	What can they do for us	Amount 5	1. Positive Pont 2. Positive Pont 3. Positive Pont	1. Negative Pont 2. Negative Pont 3. Negative Pont

Description of the partners who will contribute to the implementation of the idea into existence:

Suppliers, Manufacturers, Legal Services, Logistics, Travel and Tourism Companies, Banks, Stores (Wholesale/Retail), IT web designers and other IT services like Cloud Hosting, Translators, Developers, Designers, Charities, Schools, Farmers, Partners you need to help you deliver value to your customer segments.

7. How to Segment Targeted Groups and Why

Classifying Customers or Users into categories and clarifying the needs of each of them is very important if we do not know the people who will be affected by any crisis how will we be able to create a plan to help them.

- **Who is the Targeted Market Segment?**
  It is very important to know the target market as stated previously who will be affected by the crisis and how will it affect them. Just making a list of people will not suffice, the list should be focused and with actual numbers. First, create a market segmentation list. Once the list has been created then chose the segments that you need to focus on and not everyone.

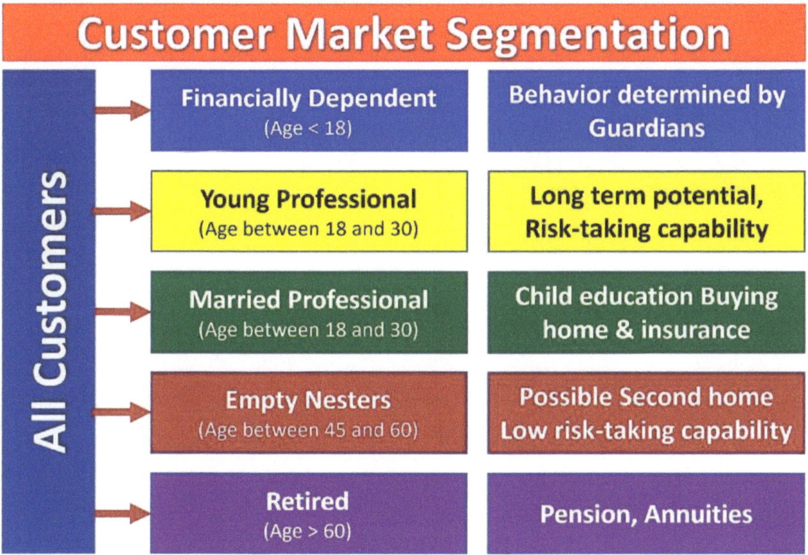

- **How many Segments do you have?**
  There are four major market segmentation groups these groups are used to ensure that the right products and or services are properly targeting the right individuals, market segmentation is about understanding customer needs and how they decide between choosing one product over another product the most important thing to remember regarding market segmentation is that some customers may want one product or service but have other needs that the product does not provide, the four market segments are: **Geographic, Demographic, Psychographic and Behavioural.**

1. **Geographic Market Segmentation**

   People in different geographic locations have cultural differences. Marketing strategists work on tailoring their products or services according to these cultural differences.

   For Example, Mcdonald's created the Veggie Burger, in India as many Indians are vegetarians so to have them come to McDonald's they had to create a new product that they did not provide before the Veggie Burger was created.

   Geographical market segmentation makes divisions based on geographical units, including:

   • Continents

   • Nations

   • Regions

   • Neighbourhoods

2. **Demographic Market Segmentation**

   Marketing strategists also use demographic segmentations.

   Creating marketing strategies based on the characteristics of customers gives organizations a better chance to meet the needs and wants of a specific group of people. As each group has different needs providing the right set of products to the right group of people is the ultimate aim of every marketing strategy.

Example: Toy manufacturers have to target kids in their advertising campaigns. Since they are the ultimate end users of the product. Creating advertisements for adults is a waste of time and money. That is why understanding your clients is very important to helping them get what they need.

Demographic variables include:

- Gender
- Age
- Income
- Socio-Economic Status
- Religion
- Race

3. **Psychographic segmentation**
Psychographic segmentation means that a person's personality influences what products or services they will be acquiring.

Psychographic segmentation strives to classify consumers based on:
- Lifestyle
- Personality
- Opinions
- Interests
- Values

This may be more difficult to achieve, as these traits may change easily and may not have readily available objective data. However, this approach may yield strongest market segment results as it groups individuals based on intrinsic motivators as opposed to external data points.

Example: A fitness apparel company may target individuals based on their interest in playing or watching a variety of sports.

4. **Behavioural Segmentation**
Behavioural segmentation is based on market data. The argument is that a customer's past actions and buying patterns are an indication of future

purchases. This is not an exact science; the risk is that customers buying habits do change over time and global events have a drastic effect over what customers will buy in the future.

EXAMPLE: During the pandemic, a lot of customers buying habits changed drastically. People started buying clothes for the home instead of clothes for parties or going to the mall. Makeup sales dropped drastically as women did not need to put on make at home. And many, many more examples.

- **Will you offer the same service to all the Segments?**
Large companies use market segmentation to focus on the marketing campaigns to the right individuals. This is also very helpful when creating a risk and crisis management plan.

  Small companies on the other hand do not have the luxury of market segmentation. They do not have a risk and crisis management plan; they just go along with the current market conditions. This is a very risky way of doing business. Many small businesses were forced to close because of the pandemic lockdown. As they were not ready for the global crisis that affected most small companies in a ruthless way.

  A total of 47% of businesses closed temporarily in 2020. Employment was down more than 54%. The companies with less than one-month liquid cash closed down completely never to open again. Companies with cash for more than 2 months were able to withstand the lockdown better. But even many of them closed down as the lockdown lasted for a lot longer than 2 months.

- **Do you have different services for each Segment?**
Does your organization have more services for different segments or do you treat all segments the same. Most companies have only one way of treating customers. They do not recognize market segmentation. As that is a very expensive recognition. They cannot spend money on dividing people into categories. As it is not feasible for them and a waste of time and money. Remember if you treat everyone the same you lose customers and business. Once a company starts losing its customers they will eventually closedown.

8. What are the Communication Channels

Methods and means by which to communicate with customers

- **How To Contact Customers Informing Them of new Procedures?**
  The many channels of communication between business and customers are:
  - Emails
  - Phone Calls
  - Social Media
  - Contact Forums
  - Live Chats
  - Review Sites
  - Text Messages

- **What is the Cost of Communicating with Customers?**
  Communication Costs incurred for phone calls local and long-distance telephone calls, and the like are allowable provided that the costs are necessary, reasonable and allocated to the contract between the company and the customer.

  Another cost that most organizations do not report is poor communication costs. Organizations lose a lot of money when they have inadequate communication between management and employees, and communications between employees and customers. Poor communications cost businesses millions every year. So it is vitally important to manage communications with customers, reduce costs and find the cheapest and best communications.

- **How Many Communication Methods Do You Have?**
  As an organization needs to communicate with customers. What communication methods does your organization use? List the communication methods in a table with the most expensive method at the top and the least expensive method at the bottom. This will allow you to know what type of communication costs the most and what costs the least. When budgeting for communication costs you can create a more realistic budget.

- **Why These Methods to Communicate Where Used?**
  Ask yourself why the organization you are working for are using the current communication methods. Has it been researched, and from the research, they have discovered that these are the best communication

methods. Or they are just using these methods because they don't know any better. These are all legitimate questions that you have to look into when creating your risk and crisis management plan.

It is very important to understand why the organization you are with uses the communication methods they are currently using. I have seen many organizations use communication methods that do not help them in any way whatsoever. The problem lies with the social media marketing companies. Many organizations use marketing firms that use outdated social media platforms, and the results they achieve are mediocre. the main social media platform that these marketing companies use is Facebook, as I said previously Facebook lost a lot of credibility when they sold their customer's personal information. If these marketing firms use UpToDate social media platforms that the majority of people use, then the results would be far greater than what the organization expects.

Communicating good news or bad news it is important to use the right platform. That way you can cover a large group of people in a very fast period of time. As a risk and crisis plan manager, you have to know how to reach the largest number of people in the fastest way possible.

- **The Best Method of Communication with The Lowest Cost?**

Best Communication Channels

SNAPCHAT Communicate with teenagers and women as they are the majority users of this platform

INSTAGRAM One of the best platforms to communicate with teenagers and Adults below 50.

TWITTER To communicate with official authorities, dignitaries and parents (Mostly Men)

Tik Tok To communicate with teenagers and parents (Mostly women) as they are this platforms majority users

There are other methods but not as famous as these are or widely used. You will notice that I have not used Facebook. I believe that it is a waste of time trying to communicate with customers using Facebook as most people have stopped using Facebook completely. It is up to you to use Facebook or not I personally don't recommend it.

9. What are the Key Resources to Implement the Plan

Key Resources such as **Cognitive, Technological, Human, Financial** and **Material** resources:

- **Cognitive:** The mental and Thought process of thinking and understanding.
- **Technological:** Improvements in technical processes that increase productivity of machines.
- **Human:** The knowledge and skills enabling them to realize their potential as productive members of society.
- **Financial:** The funds needed to finance the projects and investments
- **Material:** Supplies or other consumable items used to complete tasks in the project.

- **What are the main resources of the idea?**
  This is the moment to talk about what you need to make the risk and crisis management plan come to life. What are the resources that you need, this is the time you have to list all the resources that are required for the plan to be successful. Remember to list each and every item that you need clearly and state why you need these items plainly not just, these items are needed. If management will finance the plan, they need to know why they are spending money and how much it will cost them.

- **How will you get these resources?**
  After making the list of items that you need to implement your plan what do you do next. How do you convince your listeners to give you what is needed to implement the plan. First things first. List the items needed in a very special way; first the items you have in the organization such as computers, tables, chairs, printers and so on. Then list the items needed that the organization would have to pay for. This is the difficult part. This will management setup and list as now they have to open the money belt.

- **What does each resource cost?**
It is very important to list the approximate cost. If you have the exact cost that is even better. But usually when creating a budget for the key items, most project manager work with approximate costs. This is very helpful as it saves time and energy contacting vendors. The best way to get approximate cost is to look at the prices on the internet and just put an average cost. That way if you get anything cheaper you save money on one item, then you have more money for more expensive items that you budgeted incorrectly, and the cost is more than what you budgeted for.

  Juggling the budget, is a work of art. You have to know how to play with numbers, moving an amount that is in access from one item to the next item that has a deficit amount budgeted. So be very creative when you play with numbers. I have always liked numbers; budgets have been my thing creating lists with numbers are what I like to do.

No.	Key Resources	Costs	Approximate Cost
1	Important items	Fixed year 1	US $ 000
2	Marketing and Social Media	Fixed year 1	US $ 000
3	Computers	Fixed Asset	US $ 000
4	Printer	Fixed Asset	US $ 000
5	Staff Salary	Fixed year 1	US $ 000
6	Software	Fixed year 1	US $ 000
7	Total		US $ 000

10. The Timeline to Creating the Plan

- **How much time is required to complete the project?**
You convinced the management about the plan you explained the plan you even managed to get the budget for the plan. One last thing to do,

when will the plan be in place, when can the plan be ready for implementation in case of any crisis management situation that may arise in the near or distant future. What do you have to do and when do you have to do it, to get every ready for that unwanted day.

- **How are the tasks distributed, and how long does it take to complete each task?**
  The most important thing to do is to divide the process into tasks that need to be completed to get everything ready on time. The matrix below will give you a description of how to plan the full implementation process.

Gantt Chart

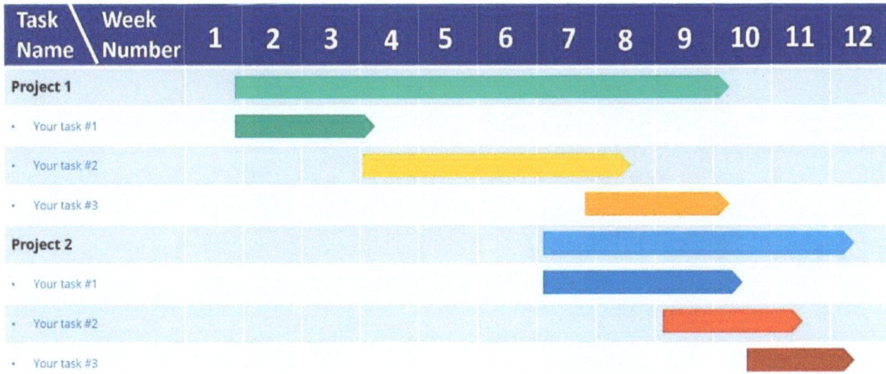

Sources of Information

- https://www.forbes.com/sites/terinaallen/2020/01/11/persuasion-how-to-convince-people-to-act-on-your-great-ideas/?sh=530ca5f7557f
- https://corporatefinanceinstitute.com/resources/knowledge/other/smart-goal/
- https://www.migso-pcubed.com/blog/pmo-project-delivery/risk-management-team-roles/
- https://marketbusinessnews.com/financial-glossary/market-segmentation/
- https://www.pnas.org/doi/10.1073/pnas.2006991117
- https://www.valuegovernance.com/tools/gantt-chart-templates/

3

Congratulations your Risk and Crisis Management Plan has been approved and now you have created the plan all the steps are in place what do you do next? This is when you have to start training your team on managing the crisis if and when it ever occurs.

Train Your Response Team on the Plan

We have Four points To Improve Crisis Management Training by using the latest Technologies.

- **Being Prepared by Using Crisis Simulations**

  With today's technology organizations can create a crisis simulation that the response team can use to practice. Crisis simulations are like computer games. There are some software that organizations can buy or rent. These software can create a mock crisis that the response team can work on and solve the problem ASAP.

  The good thing about these software's is that they are not very expensive, and you don't need a large budget to use them. They give you the ability to see firsthand what a real crisis can look like and work as a team to solve the crisis situation as fast as possible.

  There are many crisis situations that can arise. An example is ransomware. A hacker can take control of your data and hold it for ransom for an amount of money. So, this is a Crisis situation you do not have access to your company data or your client's data. What do you do. The simulation will help you and your response team solve the problem before it can turn into a reality. Your team can go through the steps and come up with solutions to a problem that many organizations have faced in the past as they were not prepared to face such a problem. Many organizations have been hacked using ransomware. The problem is that even if you pay the ransom to release your data, you cannot be sure this will not happen again as many hackers create back doors so they can enter your system again and again.

- **Motivating Staff and Keeping Them Engaged**
Gone are the days when staff members were asked to read a book on the process of crisis management. It is boring and most people do not like reading. The good thing about using technology to create a mock crisis situations is that staff members get to work on a problem and come up with practical solutions to the problems that can be implemented on the spot. This sort of team collaboration creates a sense of team spirit within the organization and it helps to increase staff motivation as they feel needed and that their ideas have value.

   When each team member has a specific task to perform during the crisis this helps them to remember what steps need to be taken at exactly the right time. The saying practice makes perfect is very true as when your team practices what they have to do they will not forget the steps so easily if they just have to read it from a manual.

- **Creating the Right Training Program**
Large organizations have a bigger number of treats that they may face in the near or distant future. Choosing the correct training method is very important. Training employees on every crisis situation is very difficult. So, what do you do? The Risk and Crisis Manager must choose the important risks and or crisis that the organization is more likely to face with a higher percentage rate of occurrence. The risks that have a lower occurrence percentage rate can be temporarily put on hold until such time as it is possible to have your response team get trained on them.

   Your response team have to be able to communicate with each other and the rest of the organization very fast so how can you achieve this? One way with today technology you can create a mobile app that all your staff have to download onto their mobiles. The response team has the ability to upload data and information onto the app. While the rest of the employees are able to receive instructions and information so that they can work together on solving the problem.

The mobile application can have information such as Crisis Manuals, Checklists, maps, safety procedures, staff contact information. Response team contact information, communication plans in case of a crisis, maps of some important locations that employees can work from incase of a crisis situation. The response team has the ability to choose what information they would like to share with the other staff members.

Using mobile apps can make staff training easier as staff members do not need to be at work to conduct a mock crisis training they can do it from anywhere as a crisis can happen at any given time of day.

- **The Best Way to Prepare for Crisis Communication**
With today's technology, all mobiles are minicomputers, using mobile phones as the new means to communicate, plan and execute all Risk and crisis management situations the best way for the present and future of the company. Having team members practice all mock training programs on their mobile phones is the way to go. It helps the response teams to practice at any time they feel necessary. Without interrupting their actual work in the organizations.

For example if a crisis situation occurs and people cannot get to the office what do they do? If the organization has a mobile app. This will help all staff members communicate with each other through the mobile application and the response teams can give instructions to staff members through the mobile app. The is the best crisis communication method with the current technology. In the future we may have more advanced ways to communicate. But that is in the future.

Having all information necessary documents, plans and procedures on the mobile application is the best way to be ready for any crisis situation. The response teams can have full access to any information, share plans with the concerned staff members. As well as have quicker and more streamlined documents and any updates. The most important thing to remember is that if a crisis situation does occur, the organizations management will feel very safe in knowing that the employees are well trained to respond to any given crisis. With the best communication technology in the palm of their hands.

Creating an Incident Command System

A number of large organizations use an Incident Command System (ICS) this system is a very effective system for any type of crisis incident or preparing the response team to manage the crisis incident. There are a number of different ICS systems that all perform similar tasks. Having an Incident Command System gives an organization an incredible advantage to surviving a major crisis event. This will increase the ability of the organization to limit financial losses and improve the organizations reputation and reduce brand name damage.

ICS is a very organized system. It helps the response team to be organized well before a crisis situation can ever start. This helps the response team save time, especially during the starting stage of a crisis situation. This system has the ability to gauge the severity of the crisis event. Is this a level 1 or level 2 or even a level 5. The great thing about this system is that it can remain functioning for long periods of time without any problems.

The ICS can be used for a different number of crisis situations example it can be used for unexpected or abrupt crisis situations such as (earthquake, Tsunami, Fire, Gas Explosion and or Landsides). Then there are business disasters that could become dangerous crisis situations for organizations such as (Cyber-attack, Ransomware, IT Data Loss, Customer Death using a Company Product, Employee Strike, Factory Shutdown and many more…)

Authenticating the Response Plan and Team Members

The crisis readiness is a never-ending cycle. It is a constant improvement process, the most important thing confirm the response plan and the response team members. There is an important thing to also remember, that every team member must have a backup person, this backup person must full knowledge of the team member's tasks, so if the original team member is not able to perform any of his or her tasks the backup person must be able to takeover without any problems.

The crisis management team must first start practicing together using a laptop or a desktop computer. The better they get the stress level has to be increased using better technologies and more complex scenarios, at the end they should be able to respond to a full-scale mock exercise. This will help uncover any problems or gaps in the plan. This will provide the team with the necessary abilities they need manage the crisis and create a team spirit the is very important in such situations, the team are able to work together as one.

Review and Update the Plan Once a Year

It is always important to remember that all business processes are not perfect they need to be regularly checked and updated. It is recommended that a full review of the crisis plan should be done once a year. This review will help in identifying any gaps in the crisis management plan and fill in those gaps or issues that could happen during an actual crisis or disaster.

Having the response team conduct an annual mock exercise of the crisis management plan will help in identifying any potential issues in the plan. Also, with the advent of new technologies and systems. Having the response team use these new systems and technologies on a yearly basis will help the team be completely UpToDate with the latest technologies. Also, with new technologies, you have new and better ways to respond to crisis situations that were not available in the past. This will help the project manager update the methods of response with the latest technologies.

Example of new technologies, WhatsApp was created in 2009. So, before 2009 how did people send text messages to each other? We had Blackberry and SMS. They were expensive and not many people could afford them. But now we can send text messages to each other in an instant and its free. So, every couple of years a new technology comes to life and our lives are changed forever. Similarly, new technologies can and will help in managing crisis situations, the most important thing to remember is that we have to be open to these technologies and not reject them just because they are new. I have seen many organizations lose a lot of money because they were not willing to change their method of doing things using new technologies. Remember change is good and profitable because nothing ever stays the same.

Remember keep evaluating the process and the changes in the process. This is the best way to learn if the changes that were made to the plan actually work better than before or not.

Learning from Mock Exercises

Remember after running your mock exercises, it is very important to interview the response team members, you have to document what they have learnt. Remember if you don't ask you will never learn. Ask your team questions like:

- What was the overall impression of how the team functioned together did they function as one or where there any problems between the team members?

- Did the team members perform a particular task well, How did they perform and what did they do?

- Did they find any areas of the plan that was unclear or hindered their work? What was it? do they know why and how they could make it better?

- Are there any specific actions that should be changed in the current plan? Why should you make the changes? And what should be the new changes?

Sources of Information

- https://www.rockdovesolutions.com/blog/4-ways-to-improve-crisis-management-training-with-technology
- https://preparedex.com/6-steps-creating-capable-crisis-management-team/